Original title:
The Ocean's Echo

Copyright © 2025 Creative Arts Management OÜ
All rights reserved.

Author: Arabella Whitmore
ISBN HARDBACK: 978-1-80587-238-2
ISBN PAPERBACK: 978-1-80587-708-0

Echoes of Distant Shores

The waves all giggle with salty cheer,
Their ticklish splashes, oh my dear!
A fish wearing glasses swims by my feet,
Says, "You should dive in, it's quite a treat!"

Bright crabs dance sideways, a quirky sight,
Waving their claws with pure delight.
A seaweed hat on a jellyfish's head,
Says, "I'm dressed for a party, come join my bed!"

A dolphin laughs, plays peek-a-boo,
With flip-flops on, just to impress you.
The seagulls caw in a karaoke show,
Singing off-key, but they steal the show!

So come grab a beach ball, let's all play fair,
With oceanic shenanigans filling the air.
Splashing and laughing till the day is done,
Nothing beats fun in the sun, oh what fun!

Blending with the Blue

Blue crabs mix paint, creating a scene,
While fish throw confetti like they're in a dream.
Seashells gossip, they're snug in the sand,
Whispering secrets, all perfectly planned!

Starfish do cartwheels, they twist and they twirl,
While sea cucumbers dance and give a whirl.
A stingray jokes about pranks in the tide,
"Watch out for waves when I suddenly glide!"

Turtles ride waves, like surf pro champs,
With shades on their eyes, they strike funny poses.
As octopuses juggle, in a comedy spree,
The laughter's contagious, yes, it's quite free!

So join in the fun, with a splash and a cheer,
For this ocean's party is the best of the year.
With humor and joy in the sea's vast embrace,
Where giggles and waves dance in perfect grace!

Coral Chorus

Underwater, fish take a dance,
Seaweed sways, giving it a chance.
Crabs do the cha-cha, shells on display,
While octopuses juggle, come join the ballet.

Turtles in sunglasses, looking so bright,
Say, 'What's up, jellyfish? Ready for flight?'
Starfish applaud with their five-pointed hands,
As the clownfish crack jokes about sandy bands.

Serenity of the Shoreline

Seagulls squawk jokes while they dive for fries,
Surfboards tumble like comedic spies.
Kids build sandcastles, yelling with glee,
But a wave rolls in, and down goes the spree.

Shells tell tales of the beach's past,
Of flip-flops lost and picnics amassed.
With every splash, laughter fills the air,
As sunburned tourists forget their despair.

The Song of Storms

Thunder grumbles, the sky wears a frown,
Dolphins invest in a little rain clown.
Waves toss seaweed like confetti galore,
While fishermen giggle, it's an aquatic score.

Lightning takes selfies, striking a pose,
With jellyfish photobombing, who knows?
"Don't worry," says the shark, "I've got my sunscreen!"
Aquatic irony—who ever saw such a scene?

Ebb and Flow

The tide comes in with a knock and a wink,
Shells all gather around for a drink.
While jellyfish bop to a beat of the sea,
Crabs throw a party—it's wild and free!

As waters retreat, they play hide and seek,
Mermaids giggle from behind a creek.
"Oh no!" shouts a flounder, "I'm late for my show!"
While sand dollars cheer, "You've got time, just go!"

Rhythms of the Tide

A lobster danced in a shell so grand,
He slipped on seaweed, we all understand.
Seagulls squawked, they thought it was rude,
But the crabs just clapped for his silly mood.

With beach balls bouncing and flip-flops in flight,
A fish tried to juggle, what a funny sight!
The waves laughed loud, a gurgling cheer,
As the tide kept rolling, bringing joy and beer.

Shores of Solitude

A lonely starfish, all quiet and blue,
Wrote poems to shells, that's what they do.
The seagulls giggled, the sand tickled toes,
While dolphins played charades, striking silly poses.

The sunbathers snored, lost in their dreams,
As crabs formed a band with shells as their teams.
They played all day, the tunes got quite loud,
While the ocean just winked, feeling quite proud.

Reflections in the Riptide

A fish with a mustache swam by with a grin,
He told all the waves, 'Hey, let's dive in!'
They splashed and they tumbled, oh what a scene,
With a squid juggling clams, it was a routine.

The tide brought a message, it rolled on the sand,
'No diving too deep, just be cool and grand.'
But a seal in a hat said, 'Let's take a chance!'
And they twirled in the ripples, joined in the dance.

The Stillness Between Waves

In the calm of the calm, a crab made his stand,
Wearing sunglasses, he felt pretty grand.
He practiced his pose for the Instagram feed,
While the fish rolled their eyes, 'What a silly breed!'

The seaweed giggled, tickling sands,
As the waves whispered jokes, formando tiny bands.
'Why don't we surf?' asked a clam with delight,
But the jellyfish yawned, 'Not tonight, we take flight!'

Song of the Rising Tide

The waves they dance with glee,
Seagulls squawk in harmony.
Each splash is like a cheer,
As crabs pinch toes, oh dear!

Sandcastles rise high and proud,
Till a wave comes thundering loud.
Down they crash, a sandy fall,
As beachgoers laugh through it all!

Surfboards crash, oh what a sight,
Wipeouts bring such sheer delight.
A dolphin's leap or fishy joke,
Nature's laughter, never broke!

So let the tide roll on with cheer,
With beach ball antics far and near.
We'll giggle as we chase our hats,
In the silly dance with friendly splats!

Chants of the Salty Air

The breeze brings whispers and tales,
Of wandering fish with silly scales.
Lobsters wear their fancy hats,
While clams just sit, no need for chats!

Collecting shells that sing and hum,
A crab may steal my sandwich, yum!
Jellyfish float with endless grace,
But watch your step, or lose your place!

Starfish claiming beachside thrones,
Pretend they're kings, all made of bones.
An octopus waves its arms so wide,
Challenging all the waves that bide!

So raise a toast to seaweed's flair,
With tasty snacks from salty air.
Together we'll laugh, dance, and twirl,
In the joyous tide, let's give it a whirl!

The Call of Distant Shores

A message floats on the salty breeze,
From faraway lands and foreign keys.
Whale songs echo, a comical tune,
They sing of fish feasts under the moon!

Pirates laughing as they set sail,
Searching for treasures, fussing without fail.
Their maps all point to the wrong little isle,
As dolphins giggle, oh what a style!

Mermaids comb seashells with flair,
But snag their hair in the ocean's chair.
They splash and giggle, what a sight,
With fishy friends, they dance all night!

So heed the call from waves that crash,
In frothy fun, let's make a splash.
Together we wander from shore to shore,
With laughter echoing forevermore!

Murmurs of the Nautical Realm

In the depths where bubbles rise,
Fish wear glasses, oh what a surprise!
A clam reads gossip from the sand,
As seabeds giggle, oh so grand!

Octopuses juggle, oh what a show,
While seahorses gossip, all in a row.
Crabs do a two-step, quite out of time,
As they dance along to bubblegum rhyme!

Waves relay news with foam and spray,
Of fishy pranks that made their day.
Turtles compete in a slow-motion race,
Leaving the souped-up dolphins in space!

So laugh with the sea, its charm and cheer,
With stories told for all to hear.
In the nautical realm, the fun is clear,
With joy in the waves and love in the sphere!

Voices of the Deep

Whales are singing, what a sight,
Seagulls are laughing, oh what a fright.
A crab in a tux, he struts with glee,
Inviting the fish to a grand jamboree.

Starfish hold meetings on rocks with flair,
While dolphins show off with acrobatic air.
A jellyfish dances, a wobbly twirl,
As clams share stories of their underwater world.

Barnacles gossip, clinging to hulls,
While octopuses prank with their slippery pulls.
A lobster's got jokes, he's quite the comedian,
Sending waves of laughter across the medians.

Mermaids are laughing, sipping on foam,
Building their castles, so far from home.
The sea's full of humor, if you just want to peek,
It's a party down here, quite unique!

Driftwood Dreams

Driftwood is lounging, taking a nap,
While old bottles gossip about their mishap.
A sandcastle king, with a crown made of shells,
Proclaims every wave to be ringing bells.

Seashells collect tales of ships that have passed,
Whispering secrets of battles amassed.
A crab with a monocle reads the day's news,
Critiquing the tides on the evening cruise.

Fish throw a party beneath the bright moon,
Clownfish are dancing—oh, what a tune!
Conch shells are booming, announcing the fun,
While a starfish DJ says, "Let's all run!"

Seagulls are squawking, the party's alive,
With plankton and seaweed, we'll all take a dive.
Driftwood dreams sway with the currents of cheer,
In this whimsical world, let's all raise a beer!

Hushed Waves at Dusk

The tide comes in, with whispers so sly,
A sea turtle chuckles, he gives it a try.
Conversations are brewing with crabs and the sand,
With fish playing poker, just as they planned.

Stars twinkle above, but the real show's below,
A group of sea cucumbers put on a glow.
They stretch and they wiggle, a spectacle grand,
While plankton take center stage, a fanciful band.

A clamshell chorus hums soft lullabies,
Giggling sea horses watch with wide eyes.
The dolphins dive deep, and the otters all splash,
Flinging the seaweed, making quite the crash.

As night settles in, the ocean now sighs,
Echoing laughter beneath darkening skies.
In the hush of the waves, joy comes to play,
Under complex stars, they dream night away!

The Sound of Solitude

A lone fish floats by with a skeptical air,
"What's with the waves? They don't seem to care."
An old shipwreck grumbles, full of old grease,
"Once I had a crew, now I'm just peace."

Barnacles whisper, sticking tight to the past,
While sea sponges wonder how long they can last.
A clam in a shell can't stop fidgeting, see,
"I'd give anything for a bit of sweet tea!"

Lobsters complain about times that are rough,
"I miss the old days, when the sea was more tough!"
While eels plug their ears, dodging all the noise,
Saying, "This solitude's just not our choice."

But still in the quiet, there's laughter to find,
Just listen real close, be patient and kind.
For every sweet sigh, there's a giggle nearby,
In the sound of the silence, joy floats on by!

Saltwater Serenade

A seagull stole my sandwich, what a prank,
I chased it down, but it just flew, clank!
The waves laughed at my flailing feet,
Oh salty breeze, you think it's a treat.

The fish below are having a ball,
Throwing seaweed like a beachy shawl.
I slip and slide, a slapstick show,
While crabs applaud my watery woe.

The sun is my witness, shining bright,
As I play tag with waves, oh what a sight!
With splashy cheers, they call my name,
In this wet and wild, hilarious game.

With each stumble, the laughter grows,
Dancing with fishes in funny clothes.
Oh how I love this silly tide,
In the salty fun, I'll take great pride.

Secrets of the Sargasso

In the depths where seaweed grows, they say,
A treasure chest of socks lost in dismay.
Dolphins giggle at my foolish hunt,
For fashion mishaps, this place is blunt.

I met a crab with a pirate's hat,
He winked at me and said, "How 'bout that?"
With a pinch of sass, he showed me around,
Where lost things float, and laughter's abound.

Jellyfish whisper their sticky desires,
While fish gossip about our silly mishires.
I tried to dance, but slipped and fell,
Now I'm the star of this aquatic swell.

The secrets swim, they twist and twine,
Among these waves, we all align.
The Sargasso's charm makes me lose track,
Of who's the captain, and where's the snack!

Shoreline Whispers

The sand tickles my toes, what a delight,
As I chase the tide, it takes off in flight.
Seagulls squawk, they join in the race,
I trip on a shell, what a goofy face!

A crab gives me sass from his cozy den,
"You think you're smooth? Try that again!"
Shells whisper secrets as I pass by,
In this sandy sitcom under the sky.

Each wave tells a joke, rolling on high,
With sea foam giggles, they wave goodbye.
There's laughter in the breeze, just look and see,
Life on the shore is a comedy spree.

And when the tide pulls back with a cheer,
It beckons us closer, without any fear.
With every splash and playful surprise,
The shoreline whispers, where humor lies.

Currents of Connection

I went for a swim, thought I'd look cool,
But got tangled up like a fool in a pool.
The fish all laughed, threw bubbles my way,
While I floundered about, trying to play.

A whale swam by with a laugh that boomed,\n"Are you
here for the splash or just drowned?"
With flippers flapping, I joined in the fun,
Splash fights with whales, oh what a run!

Starfish cheered from their rocky shows,
As I slipped and slid, wore seaweed clothes.
"Join the dance!" they sang in a silly tone,
While I twirled around, feeling right at home.

In the currents of laughter, we connected,
With fishy friends, my spirit resurrected.
In the ocean's embrace, we find our place,
A world of giggles, joy, and salty grace.

Symphonic Surges

Waves play tambourines, so bright,
Fish dance with fins, what a sight!
Seagulls squawk a little tune,
Mermaids giggle, under the moon.

Splashing water brings delight,
Crabs wear hats, what a fright!
Starfish cheer with clenched fists,
In this world, nothing's amiss.

Whales sing low, off-key still,
Turtles skate down the hill.
Jellyfish float with pure glee,
Every splash, a symphony.

So grab your snacks, join the spree,
Laughter mingles, wild and free!
With each ripple, joy expands,
In this concert, love still stands.

Tidal Tales

Salty tales from the foam,
Octopus lost its way home.
Clams tell jokes, oh so punny,
Shrimp play tricks, all in good fun!

Seaweed parties with the tide,
Dolphins jump, their joy can't hide.
Crabs play poker on the sand,
This wild life is simply grand!

Seagulls steal a sandwich snack,
While anchovies dance a backtrack.
The tide's tales will make you smile,
Come and join us for a while!

Fishes gossip in a hole,
Oysters dream in their shell shoals.
Every ripple tells a story,
In these depths, there's much glory.

The Poetry of Plankton

Tiny stories float and twirl,
Plankton twinkle, dance, and swirl.
Bouncing here like happy beads,
In their world, there's much to heed.

Little critters on a spree,
Living life so carelessly.
The currents whisper light and quick,
Silly jokes, they share and pick.

In a drop, they start a show,
Performing tricks, oh what a glow!
Riding waves as if they're kings,
In their realm, oh how it sings!

So while you'd think they're all so meek,
They're the stars at every peak.
In this vast sea of big commotion,
Find the fun in every notion.

Murmurs of the Midnight Sea

Moonlit waters softly tease,
Crabs have parties, oh, with ease.
Whispers float on a cool breeze,
Stars wink down like a tease.

Nighttime critters start to play,
While sea otters steal the day.
Urchins tell their corny jokes,
And dancing fish, oh how it pokes!

Sailors dream of treasure maps,
While sea turtles take quick naps.
The night giggles as it sways,
In this realm of wondrous plays.

So raise a glass to midnight fun,
Where every splash says, 'We have won!'
In these murmurings of delight,
Find your joy in endless night.

Distant Horizons Call

A seagull stole my sandwich, oh dear,
Chasing it down, I lost my cheer.
Fish are laughing, splashing about,
As I yell, "Hey, bring that back, no doubt!"

The waves dance high, in a sassy sway,
Squids and crabs have joined the play.
They flip and twirl, like they're on a spree,
While I sit back, sipping salt in my tea.

Sunbathers wiggle, trying to tan,
But sand sticks to them like a clingy fan.
Seagull drops a gift, that's meant to be sweet,
But I'm here dodging what's raining from feet!

Distant horizons, what joy you bring,
With waves that dance and foolish things.
Each splash a reminder of laughter galore,
Life's just a circus, on this sandy shore.

Timeless Tides

Floats made of pool noodles and dreams,
Bouncing about, or so it seems.
Kids in the water, splashing with glee,
While adults sip cocktails, pretending to be free.

A crab pinches a toe, what a funny sight,
As beachgoers shriek in a minor fright.
Laughter erupts like the waves on the sand,
Nature's comedians, they all have it planned.

The sunburned tourists, with stripes like a zebra,
Swear they'll never forget their suntan idea.
But as they frolic, a wave gives a shout,
And bubbles up laughter, there's no doubt!

Timeless tides roll in, bringing us cheer,
With every splash, it's the best time of year.
It's a comedic ballet, under the sun,
Life's too short, let's bask and just have fun!

Moonlit Waves

Under the moon, the waves start to prance,
A fish takes a leap, like it's part of a dance.
Starfish giggle, playing it cool,
While shells gossip, right next to the pool.

"Did you see that? It's a dolphin in flight!"
They chatter and squeal, what a magical sight.
Mermaids are sunbathing, with a wink and a grin,
While the octopus joins in, wearing a fin.

The tide rolls in, setting the stage,
For crustacean skits and an octopus page.
Laughter bubbles up, with each crashing wave,
In this odd aquatic world, we're all feeling brave.

Moonlit waves, oh what a delight,
With the beach full of creatures that glow in the night.
Let's gather round, let our worries unwind,
In this silly paradise, joy we will find!

Fluid Conversations

A whale and a turtle share tales so grand,
While a crab tells jokes about life on land.
Fish roll their eyes, they're just not amused,
While dolphins toss seaweed, looking so confused.

"Why did the dolphin bring a snorkel?" a fry,
"Because he was tired of swimming on high!"
The ocean's a stage, where laughter's the goal,
With humor as deep as the sea takes a stroll.

Jellyfish jive in electric hues,
While whales sing low in the night, what's the news?
Stars twinkle brightly, the audience roars,
As each wave of laughter opens new shores.

Fluid conversations, let laughter ensue,
In this underwater world, where fun's always true.
Join the sea creatures, hear their silly views,
In this vast ocean, we'll share joyful blues!

Beneath the Surface Sound

Under the waves, fish play hide and seek,
A guppy's giggle, the dolphins squeak.
Seagulls drop snacks from their high-flying flight,
Tuna try dancing, but can't get it right.

A crab throws a party, wearing a hat,
While starfish are lounging, thinking, "What's that?"
A whale tells a joke, the corny old kind,
But all of his buddies are way too blind.

The seaweed sways, joins in on the fun,
With currents that swirl like a dance on the run.
Bubbles are popping, laughter reaches the sky,
Who knew sea life could be this spry?

Underwater concerts, a splashy ballet,
Octopus conductors lead the fish ballet.
With fins flapping rhythm, they boogie and glide,
While crabs click their claws, they dance with pride.

Serenade of the Sea

Turtles sing sweetly, in harmonic glee,
While little fish jest, "Can you dance like me?"
The sandcastles giggle, washed down by the tide,
As waves hum a tune of a wild, funny ride.

Seashells hold secrets of all that we seek,
A clam whispers softly, "Hey, I'm not meek!"
The sea cucumbers chuckle, rolling about,
And garden of coral joins in with a shout.

A plankton parade in their mini parade,
They twirl and they swirl, in sunlight displayed.
The kelp starts to shimmy, sways to the beat,
While crabs on the sidelines tap danced with their feet.

With bubbles of laughter, perform a grand show,
The fishes all cheer, "Come on! Let's go!"
A party in the deep, where no grump can stay,
Underwater talent, it's a splashy ballet!

Ripples of Reflection

As waves laugh and giggle, they tickle the shore,
Sea turtles glide past, like an ocean encore.
Seagulls attempt dives, but just float with a plop,
And crabs scuttle sideways, "We just can't stop!"

Starfish offer high fives, "Hey, buddy, you there?"
While clams roll their eyes, "Do they even care?"
The jellyfish jiggles, a jiggly old fool,
As currents keep swirling, breaking the rule.

Dolphins dive deep, with a splash and a cheer,
Echoing laughter, filling up the clear.
With shells painted bright, tiny homes on display,
They chat and they chuckle, through night and through day.

With laughter as buoyant as foam on the crest,
Every fish in the sea feels utterly blessed.
Because even underwater, even in the blue,
Silly shenanigans will always shine through!

Depths of Distant Dreams

In the depths, fish dream of a floaty parade,
With jellybeans swirling, their sweet escapade.
Whales serenade bubbles, humming a tune,
While sea urchins chuckle, "We'll dance 'til noon!"

A treasure chest opens, spilling goldfish galore,
While octopuses plan for a feast by the shore.
Squids are the chefs, shaking up at the grill,
Believing their cooking fits every fish's thrill.

Eels whisper secrets in shadows so dark,
While shrimps bust a move, breaking out of the park.
The currents are filled with a shimmer of zest,
As mermaids come twirling, "Our party is best!"

Late-night tales of krakens, they're not what they seem,
With twinkling lights shining, fulfilling each dream.
So dive into laughter, the ocean's delight,
Where smiles and giggles stay bright through the night!

Currents of Forgotten Dreams

Bubbles rise and tickle toes,
As fish parade in sequined clothes.
They wiggle, they dance, such a sight,
Who knew sea creatures could be so bright?

A crab wears shades, looking so cool,
While mermaids laugh, breaking the rule.
Their laughter echoes, a splashing sound,
In a party where fish spin round and round.

Starfish play cards on a sandy bed,
While seaweed wiggles, shaking its head.
A dolphin jokes, with a wink so sly,
He says, "Why not take a dip? Oh my!"

The tides sigh softly, with playful tunes,
As sea cucumbers hum under moons.
In currents of dreams, they frolic and swirl,
Forget the world, let the laughter unfurl.

Harmonies of the Deep Blue

Octopuses juggling with flair so divine,
Clownfish cracking jokes, sipping on brine.
Anemone blooms, shaking its fronds,
While turtles bob like living beyonds.

A seahorse frets over a missed date,
With a flounder who just can't relate.
They share tales of missed love in the tide,
As jellyfish sway like they're on a ride.

A fish flips out, claiming he's lost,
In schools of bass, just a bit of a cost.
"Got GPS?" the snail is asked with glee,
He chuckles and shrugs, "Just follow me!"

In the deep blue, life is a jest,
With bubbles and giggles, it's all for the best.
So join in the fun, dance with delight,
The ocean's a stage, on every night.

Rhythms Cradled by the Shore

Seagulls chat like gossiping friends,
As sea foam dances and laughter blends.
Sandcastles crumble, a kingdom's fall,
With a wave's gentle push, they vanish, all!

A starfish complains of his lack of shoes,
While crabs throw a dance party, spreading good news.
"Ballet in the tide, the crabs call it fun,
Just try not to step on the sand dollars, hon!"

The tide rolls in, like a playful breeze,
Tickling the toes of sunbathers with ease.
A clam reads a book, says it's quite a tale,
About a fish who dreamed of sailing a sail.

At sunset, the beach is a stage for the absurd,
With rock pools reflecting the antics unheard.
So come and join in, where the laughter is pure,
The rhythms of joy, a delightful allure.

Secrets Carried by the Wind

Seagulls whisper secrets to ships passing by,
As waves roll their eyes with a dramatic sigh.
Fish are in on it, dressed in disguise,
Playing hide and seek, while the sun starts to rise.

Underwater pirates with fake golden teeth,
Count their treasures, hiding beneath.
A mermaid with sass sings songs oh so bold,
"Who needs a treasure? I've got tales to be told!"

The wind plays tricks with the jellyfish float,
Sending them swirling like a circus boat.
"Catch me if you can!" the clumsy ones shout,
As they flip and they flop, with a splashing route.

Secrets are swirling in mists at dusk,
With laughter and giggles amidst the husk.
So let's share our stories, let's tell them at night,
Where whispers of fun make the world feel just right.

The Call of Distant Shores

A crab just called me a nice big snack,
But I'm much too smart for that tasty hack.
I waved with a shell, just to tease his eye,
As he flipped his claws, I danced right by.

The seagulls squawked a comedy show,
As fish collaborated below in a row.
I laughed so hard that I fell in the sand,
But that sneaky sand crab had a sneaky hand.

Coral reefs laughed with colors so bright,
As I tried to catch a fish, oh what a sight!
They donned little hats and quite fancy shoes,
While teasing my efforts, they couldn't lose.

So when next you wander by the shore's glee,
Remember the laughter, the jokes, and the spree.
For nature's a stage where all creatures play,
A giggle-filled gala on a sunny day.

Waves of Introspection

In deep blue waters, the fish all muse,
What's better, swimmin' or makin' the news?
A dolphin pondered with wisdom so rare,
As stingrays giggled, floating without care.

A clam wrote a novel, a real page-turner,
But let out a whisper, 'I'm such a slow learner!'
With pearls of wisdom hidden inside,
While octopuses laughed, they took it in stride.

The turtles debated who's fastest and best,
While sea urchins crowded, pretending to test.
But who wins the race, oh the ponderous game,
When the winner just naps? It's all the same!

So here in the tides, deep thoughts and reflections,
Flow like the surf, in whimsical sections.
It's a comedy show, if you look closely,
Even deep thoughts can swim just a bit coastily.

Songs of the Serene

A fish took the stage with a mic made of sea,
Sang ballads of bubbles, oh so carefree.
While clams clapped along with a rhythm so grand,
A seaweed dancer twirled, just as they planned.

Jellyfish floated, their glow a delight,
With each sway they performed, a dazzling sight.
The crabs played the drums, while barnacles cheered,
And every odd note was gladly endeared!

Starfish threw petals, as bright as the sun,
While everyone laughed, had so much fun.
Barnacle bands rocked out under the waves,
In this joyous concert, no one misbehaves.

So join in the chorus, let laughter be heard,
For nature's the symphony, let's sing out a word.
A melody woven from seaweed and foam,
Is a funny reminder of our ocean home.

Beneath the Surface

Submersed in the chaos of fishy ballet,
Where bubbles are giggles and currents play.
A treasure chest laughed as it opened wide,
Finding lost trinkets that fish had denied.

The sharks held a meeting, dark suits in place,
Discussing their dinner, with a serious face.
But when one lost a tooth, oh what a scene,
They burst into chuckles, humor pristine.

The sea cucumbers, wise and austere,
Held their own council with no liquid fear.
In their slow-motion waddle, they offered wise fun,
While the clownfish giggled, enjoying the pun.

So here lies the magic, beneath foamy swirls,
Where laughter is hidden in aquatic twirls.
Each creature conveys what's fun in their own,
For there under waves, all hearts feel at home.

Currents of Memory

Splashing waves dance with glee,
Fishes wear hats, oh can't you see?
Seagulls in disco moves they sway,
Tickling the beachgoers' feet today.

Starfish hold a talent show,
While crabs strut down the catwalk in tow.
A dolphin jokes, flips, and slides,
Echoes of laughter the sea abides.

Shells gossip secrets of ages past,
Whispers of adventures—oh, what a blast!
Mermaids giggle with a splash and a wiggle,
As the tide ebbs, the sand begins to jiggle.

Memory flows like the sea's own tide,
With a splash, we embrace the joy inside.
A boat sails in, its anchor set free,
To laugh with the waves on this jolly spree.

Nautical Reverberations

A crab wearing glasses tells quite a tale,
While octopuses juggle with style and detail.
Fish in tuxedos swim by with a wink,
As bubbles of laughter rise up and think.

Lighthouses chuckle at ships going past,
And seaweed dances, a party unsurpassed.
Captain's hat on a seagull's head,
Makes you wonder what's been said.

Barnacles form a rock band tight,
Playing tunes that keep us up all night.
The rhythm of waves joins in the fun,
While sunbathing starfish soak in the sun.

With every splash, a chuckle rolls out,
Nature's humor leaves us in doubt.
As bubbles rise under the moon's soft grin,
Nautical whispers invite us to join in.

Songs from the Abyss

Deep down where shadows play,
A chatty eel has much to say.
Crabs sing songs of old folklore,
While sea cucumbers share tales galore.

The angler fish winks with a light,
Says, "Join our dance, it's a real delight!"
Squids squirt ink in a playful spree,
Creating portraits of you and me.

In the twilight zone where laughs descend,
Merfolk hold a party with no end.
Jellyfish float like balloons in the air,
Tickling the fins of all who dare.

Notes bubble up from the ocean's deep,
Wisdom and jokes the creatures keep.
With every wave, an echo we find,
Humor of the sea, gentle and kind.

Salted Breeze Lullaby

Salted air carries giggles and sighs,
As seagulls play peek-a-boo in the skies.
Waves crash softly on the sandy shore,
Tickling toes forevermore.

Frogs in the tidal pools sing out loud,
While seashells form an applause so proud.
A fish in a tux drops the perfect beat,
As the tide rolls in, it feels so sweet.

Surfboards ride the fun-filled waves,
Mermaids wave flags like little braves.
With sandy cheeks and sun-kissed hair,
We're lost in the joy, without a care.

Underneath the waves, laughter will glide,
Salted breeze wraps us, a giggling tide.
As the sun sets low, it whispers a rhyme,
Our joyful hearts beat to ocean's chime.

Fluid Footprints

Footprints in the sand, they slip and slide,
Sandy toes dancing, it's a funny ride.
Crabs in tuxedos, they join the fun,
Pinching at your ankles, oh what a run!

Seagulls are squawking, their laughter loud,
Stealing my chips, they're such a crowd.
Surfboards are wobbly, I'm taking a spill,
A splashy retirement, gives me a thrill!

Flip-flops are flying, and so is my hat,
Splashing around like a giant cat.
Dolphins are giggling, giving a cheer,
While I'm in the water, letting go of my fear!

So let's enjoy this clumsy spree,
Beneath the sun where we feel so free.
With laughter and splashes that never cease,
We'll make a splash, oh what a masterpiece!

Harmony of the Deep

Bubbles are giggling, just waiting to burst,
Fish in tuxedos, they're ready to first!
A seaweed symphony, off-key yet bright,
Even the octopus joins in the fight!

The clownfish are juggling, what a silly show,
While turtles just waddle, moving so slow.
The jellyfish boogie, floating with flair,
Dancing in circles, without any care!

A sea cucumber, looking quite confused,
Joining the party, they feel so amused.
With bubbles as confetti, we're spinning around,
In this underwater circus, joy knows no bound!

So come join the splashy aquatic fest,
Where laughter is plenty, and joy is the best.
Beneath the waves, we'll sing and we'll cheer,
In this hilarious dance, we've got nothing to fear!

The Language of the Deep Blue

Whales speak in riddles, it's hard to decode,
While fish tell tall tales, on their slippery road.
Starfish are gossiping, they wink at each other,
Creating great legends, like no other!

Blowfish are puffing, they think they're so grand,
While tiny shrimps giggle, they underhand.
With sea urchins grinning, looking quite coy,
Their spiky charm gives all the fish joy!

Anemones wave, but they tickle your skin,
In this undersea parlor, laughter begins.
With coral reefs chatting, in colors so bright,
They revel in stories that dance in the light!

So tune in your ears to this wacky exchange,
You'll find every sea creature is perfectly strange.
In this funny dialogue, we discover what's true,
In bubbles of laughter, we sail on the blue!

Shadows on the Sand

Footprints left behind, they dance with the tide,
Casting silly shadows where giggles reside.
A crab grabs a snack, it's a delightful sight,
While I trip on my towel, oh what a plight!

Umbrellas are spinning, taken by the breeze,
Chasing after seagulls, with utmost ease.
My sunscreen is running, a line down my face,
In all this commotion, what a goofball race!

The beach ball is bouncing, and children all cheer,
While I try to juggle – oh dear, oh dear!
A family of raccoons joins in the fray,
Stealing my snacks, they just won't obey!

As the sun sinks low, in colors so grand,
We laugh at the silliness found in the sand.
With shadows still dancing, and joy in the air,
This funny escapade is beyond compare!

The Language of Gulls

The gulls engage in chatter and squawk,
From pier to pier, they waddle and walk.
One thinks he's a sailor, wild and free,
While others just squabble for a chip from me.

They tease the dogs, they swoop and dive,
Stealing snacks, oh how they strive!
With flappy wings and cheeky grins,
These feathered jesters know they win.

In a language of squawks, they trade their tales,
While fishermen laugh at their gusty wails.
For every fish that struggles to swim,
There's a gull nearby, ready for him.

So if you wander by the shore,
And hear their jokes, just watch and roar.
For in their cries lies comic delight,
As they prance and play in the morning light.

Ebbing Secrets of the Bay

The tide rolls in with a squishy sound,
And whispers secrets all around.
With floating flotsam and bits of foam,
It tells tall tales of where it roamed.

A crab in a shell thinks he's a knight,
Yelling at waves with all his might.
While seaweed giggles and bobs in glee,
A game of tag, oh how it can be!

The fishermen chuckle, casting their nets,
While seagulls dive in, placing bets.
Will they catch dinner or just some fries?
It's all a gamble under the skies.

So next time you stroll by a bay,
Listen close; don't just walk away.
For secrets ebbing, funny and bright,
Are swirling with laughter, pure delight.

Echoes of the Untamed Tide

The wild waves crash with a thunderous roar,
Making shells dance on the sandy floor.
They swipe at beach balls with joyful glee,
"Come play with us!" they call, free and spree!

A jellyfish bobs like a quirky balloon,
While crabs strut by, feeling the tune.
They hold a parade, all colors and flair,
With wiggly tails and a splash of air.

Even the starfish plays peek-a-boo,
"Come tickle my arms; I can do it too!"
The tide giggles back with frothy embraces,
While sandcastles crumble in hilarious races.

Under the sun, life's a silly spree,
With salty frolics and glee at sea.
So join in the laughter, don't let it slide,
As nature erupts with the fun of the tide.

A Caress of Ocean's Breath

The breeze whips up with a mischievous tease,
Whispering secrets among the trees.
It picks up hats and sends them a-flying,
While seagulls dive down, giggling and trying.

A picnic spread is a feast for the glee,
But somehow the ants seem to disagree!
With sandwiches rolling and drinks on the floor,
The whole beach party turns into a chore.

The waves tumble over, a comical sight,
As kids run away with shrieks of delight.
The ocean throws giggles, it's playful and wide,
With splashes that sparkle, come join the ride!

So let's raise a cup to the fun and the froth,
To the crazy antics that nature doth cloth.
For usually calm can get quite a twitch,
With laughter echoing, each tide's little glitch.

Whispers in the Foam

Waves chat with sand, they're quite the pair,
Shells share gossip, floating through air.
Seagulls squawk jokes, dive with flair,
While starfish giggle, no need to care.

Crabs dance sideways, in a pinch they prance,
Turtles are slow, but they love to dance.
A fish slips by, in goofy pants,
Splashing and laughing, it takes a chance.

Mermaids toss seashells, what's in the news?
Seaweed's a wig, for clams to use.
The tide keeps rolling, who could refuse?
With laughter so bright, it's hard to lose.

Octopus juggles, an act to see,
With eight goofballs, it's quite the spree.
The ocean's alive, oh so carefree,
In this watery world, just let it be.

A Symphony of Surges

The waves hit the shore with a comedic splash,
Sea cucumbers giggle in a wobbly dash.
A dolphin leaps high, in quite a rash,
And fish tell tales of a sinking gash.

The tide brings tales of a whimsical show,
Where walruses dance and mermaids glow.
Sandcastles topple, they put on quite a show,
As crabs play clarinets in a row.

Seashells gossip about a whale in town,
While jellyfish wiggle, never a frown.
Sea anemones bounce, wearing their gown,
In this watery circus, never a down.

A ship goes by, and it honks a beat,
As seabirds join in, launching their greet.
The ocean's a stage, with laughter so sweet,
Creating a symphony, oh what a treat!

Currents of Calm

A hermit crab rolls in a borrowed shell,
With sniffs and snorts, it knows all too well.
A gentle breeze hums, casting a spell,
As dolphins play tag, ringing their bell.

Floating along, seaweed waves bye,
An octopus spins, showing its tie.
A school of fish dances, oh so spry,
While turtles munch snacks, waving to passersby.

The sun sets low, it gives a warm wink,
In dusk's light, we stop to think.
Seagulls swap tales over a cool drink,
And crabs take a stroll, in sync with the ink.

The horizon blushes, painted with cheer,
In this world of whimsy, we shed the fear.
With each ripple and laugh, we hold dear,
The sea makes us chuckle, soft and clear.

Beneath the Rolling Blue

Down below waves, where giggles reside,
Live creatures who dance, with nothing to hide.
Anemones sway, like they're on a ride,
While clownfish can't stop, laughing with pride.

The octopus folds, in a silly twist,
Creating a scene that cannot be missed.
With bubbles and blunders, it adds to the list,
Of antics beneath, nature's sweet tryst.

Barracudas play peek-a-boo, their eyes so wide,
And sea horses trot, like they're in a stride.
Each turn and swirl, they just can't bide,
In the depths of the blue, joy cannot hide.

An orchestra swells, with laughter and cheer,
In this ocean of antics, we lose all fear.
So dive in and join, the fun is right here,
Where every bubble pops, full of good cheer!

Twilight Tide

The seaweed dances like a wild mat,
A crab in a tux, all fancy and fat.
The waves chuckle softly, oh what a sight,
As dolphins perform in the fading light.

Seagulls are squawking, they want a free snack,
While I drop my sandwich, oh give it back!
They flap and they dive, a feathery spree,
I think they conspired, just to mess with me.

The starfish reclines, like he's on a chair,
He's wearing a smile, as if he don't care.
A hermit crab rolls, with a shell snazzy-new,
He's king of the beach, in his flashy view.

At twilight, the tide brings a giggling sound,
As the sea frolics round and plays on the ground.
With every soft ripple, I find it quite queer,
My troubles are washed, just as long as I'm here.

Dance of the Driftwood

A piece of driftwood takes center stage,
He wiggles and jiggles, oh such a sage.
With barnacles clapping, they cheer him on,
Who knew that a log could be such a con?

A starfish joins in with a funky spin,
While shells clap their hands, it's a raucous din.
The tide's the DJ, spinning beats on the shore,
And all of the sea critters can't help but adore.

A quirky old octopus twirls with great flair,
He juggles some sea cucumbers up in the air.
The fish form a line, doing the conga dance,
This underwater revelry puts me in a trance.

The driftwood bows low, the crowd begins to cheer,
With a wink and a nod, he whispers, "Bring beer!"
As waves crash with laughter, night begins to fall,
The beach holds a party, let's have a ball!

Whispering Waves

The waves whisper secrets to the sandy floor,
Telling tales of fish who've come ashore.
A clam grips its pearls, says, "I'm quite the catch,"
While a lazy old turtle looks up from his stretch.

The waves giggle softly, like kids at play,
Tickling the toes of those splashing all day.
A starfish complains, "Why can't we just drift?
I'd rather be lounging than giving a lift!"

The sea urchins snicker, oh what a crew,
As they poke at each other, it's quite the hullabaloo.
The gulls share a joke from way up high,
"Did you hear what the crab said? I nearly cried!"

With each rolling wave comes a chuckle and cheer,
As sea creatures giggle at the jokes that they hear.
The ocean's a playground with laughter in tow,
And under the surface, the fun's set to flow.

A Canvas of Ocean Sounds

The ocean paints music with each splash and swell,
A merry old tune that I know all too well.
The hiccup of bubbles and seagulls' squawk,
Create a light symphony, the beachy rock.

A fish with a hat offers me a seat,
He says, "Join my band, it'll be quite a treat!"
With conch shells as trumpets, they start the parade,
Off-beat clams clap, the rhythm they've made.

Old crabs scuttle by with a tap-tap-tap,
Trying to keep up, but they're caught in the trap.
The waves slide along like they're in on the joke,
As jellyfish giggle and start to provoke.

With each graceful ripple, the ocean does sing,
The laughter of breezes makes my heart take wing.
So let's dance through the tide, with joy all around,
In this vibrant realm where magic abounds.

A Symphony of Shells

Upon the shore, a snail marches slow,
Carrying secrets that no one will know.
A crab with a mic sings a tune so bizarre,
While seagulls critique from the roof of a car.

Starfish are clapping, their arms all askew,
As clams in the chorus crack jokes to the crew.
The tide rolls in, bringing laughter galore,
Each wave a reminder of fun evermore.

A fish with a top hat recites in a spin,
With bubbles-like laughter escaping his fin.
An octopus juggles, his skills quite impressive,
While a dolphin bursts forth, his jumps so excessive.

The beach turns a stage, with sand as the floor,
Where creatures unite, laughter's all we adore.
With giggles and splashes, the sun shines so bright,
In this whimsically silly aquatic delight!

Lullabies from the Abyss

In the dark depths, where the sea creatures glide,
A sleepy old turtle takes a cruise, it's his ride.
With bubbles for pillows, he starts to hum low,
To the rhythm of currents that softly do flow.

The anglerfish glows with a light like a show,
Singing softly to shrimp who have nowhere to go.
A chorus of eels wriggles in and out,
While a pufferfish laughs, 'What's this all about?'

A whale in the distance, a baritone king,
Rocks to the rhythm of the lullabies sing.
His friends all gather, their voices take flight,
As they float in the dark, bright stars shining bright.

Resting deep under, where the laughs never cease,
These lullabies echo, creating sweet peace.
For even the deep ocean likes to have fun,
As it rocks all its creatures 'neath the light of the sun!

Dances in the Moonlight

Under moonbeams, the waves start to sway,
Where fishes wear gowns for a sweet ballet.
A shrimp takes the lead, with moves so refined,
While jellyfish twirl, their tendrils aligned.

Seahorses whisper, "This dance is quite nice,
But watch out for crabs, they'll roll like some dice!"
Mollusks in tuxedos join in the delight,
As barnacles rock to the rhythm of night.

A dolphin appears, with a splash and a twirl,
Creating a whirl of fins, tails unfurl.
The moonlight transforms the water's fine waves,
Into a stage where the merriment braves.

With giggles and splashes beneath the dim moon,
These underwater creatures dance in full bloom.
As the night winds down, they bid their adieu,
Till tomorrow, when the dance starts anew!

Beneath the Surface

Bubbles are popping, it's quite the ballet,
A school of small fish are all dressed to play.
They waddle and wiggle, creating a scene,
As they tease the old starfish, who just wants to dream.

An octopus laughs with a wink and a grin,
"A tickle, dear fish? Ready? Let's begin!"
And with a quick swipe of his eight wiggly limbs,
The little ones giggle, like joyful little Sims.

Clams snap their shells, keeping time with the beat,
While sea cucumbers wriggle their feet.
The jellies all float, in a whimsical trance,
Join hands, (or appendages), for a merry dance.

Underwater drama, all bubbles and glee,
Where the fish cast a spell, like a school's jubilee.
With each gentle swoosh, the laughter takes flight,
Beneath this vast sea, everything feels right!

Stories Flow

The waves have tales, they whisper and giggle,
Of shipwrecks and treasures that lie just a wiggle.
Shells with big ears listen close to the tale,
Of pirates who argued under the bright sail.

A lobster with sass recounts a great fight,
With a clam that declared it was out of his sight.
Seagulls overhead chirp out their opinions,
While the crabs pass around popcorn as minions.

Anemones dance to the story's own beat,
As each side dish of laughter feels oh-so-complete.
The waters are alive, with fun to be found,
In this bubbling realm, where joy knows no bounds.

So gather 'round listeners, the tales now unfurl,
From the sands to the tides, let laughter swirl.
For each grain of sand holds a story so grand,
And here in the waves, together we stand!

Currents of the Heart

Waves crash down, I take my stand,
Fish are dancing, oh so grand!
My toes are wet, my hair is frizzy,
Why's the sea acting all so dizzy?

Seagulls squawk, they steal my snack,
Oh no, there goes my sandwich pack!
Dolphins giggle, flip and dive,
While I'm just trying to survive!

Sand between my toes, it's quite the mess,
Shells are treasures, I must confess!
But every wave that pulls me down,
Makes me laugh, I'm still the clown!

The tide rolls in with such a flair,
Splashing water everywhere!
With every chuckle, I shout with glee,
"Who's the captain? It's totally me!"

Harmonies in the Deep

Crabs are scuttling, pinching tight,
Shrimps are jamming, feeling bright!
An octopus plays the saxophone,
While I'm just trying not to moan.

A whale sings bass, it's quite a treat,
While starfish dance, looking so sweet!
In water ballet, I've got two left feet,
My flopping moves can't be beat!

A sea turtle rolls, and I just stare,
Thinking, "Wow, I should try that dare!"
But as I wobble, flop, and twist,
Oh no! My sunglasses met the mist!

With laughter loud, we're all in sync,
Living boldly, with no time to think!
In the depths where the funny flows,
Even the seaweed strikes a pose!

Celestial Sea Sounds

Bubbles pop and laughter churns,
Cosmic rays in waves that turn!
Crashing laughter, sounds profound,
Mermaids giggling all around!

A starfish sings a tune so weird,
A fish that snorts, I can't believe!
Even the jellyfish join the fun,
In this crazy aquatic run!

Under moonlight, the dolphins race,
But watch your snacks—don't lose your face!
With every splash and silly glide,
Joy spins fast on this salty ride!

In the twilight, we're all aglow,
Making memories in the flow!
What a blast, this cosmic play,
Splashing joy at the end of the day!

The Siren's Song

A siren's laugh, it fills the air,
With a wink and wave, she's found the flair!
But don't be fooled by her sweet hum,
This sea witch's tea is far from yum!

Fishes wiggle, dance with glee,
While I am stuck in seaweed spree!
With every note, I lose my shoe,
What a sight, oh who knew?

Seashells clatter as the ocean sings,
Dancing crabs wear tiny rings!
When I jump in for my next big splash,
I hope my phone doesn't crash!

Laughter echoes, waves on repeat,
Making a symphony, oh so sweet!
As I paddle and splash till dusk,
I'm the captain of this funny husk!

Secrets in the Brine

In the wave's quick dance, fish gossip a tale,
Old crab outsmarted, now wears a big veil.
Seaweed's a wig, quite the stylish display,
While starfish think they can twirl and sway.

Jellyfish wiggled, they think they're so grand,
But ended up stuck in a drifting old band.
Seagulls are laughing, they're never quite nice,
Stealing fries from the beach, oh, isn't that slice?

The turtle keeps snoring, he dreams of a race,
While dolphins perform with a splash and a chase.
Barnacles cling like that friend who won't leave,
Planned a big party, but forgot to retrieve!

The ocean's a riddle, a treasure to find,
With crusty old secrets and giggles entwined.
Splash in for laughter, let worries just fade,
For the sea keeps on chuckling, in frolics we wade.

Underwater Reveries

Down in the deep, where the bubbles do giggle,
A fish told a joke, and it made the snail wiggle.
The octopus juggles, with eight arms in flight,
While shrimp in tuxedos are ready to bite.

Eels lend an ear, with a fair share of sass,
As sea cucumbers try to join in the class.
Starfish play poker, they're good at the bluff,
But they never can share — oh, that's just too tough!

Puffers inflate, thinking they're quite the sight,
While clowns throw a party with colors so bright.
Whales sing a tune, sound waves fill the scene,
As seals bring the snacks, oh, they're on the cuisine!

Coral reefs cheer, with a picnic of fun,
Underwater games leave everyone spun.
Join in the laughter, let joy intertwine,
In the sea's crazy world, the jokes are divine.

Echoing Shells

Shells on the shore, they gossip and squeak,
Tales of the kraken that never dare peek.
"Did you hear about Herman, the clam with a grin?
He's been on a diet — just plankton and gin!"

Seagulls squawk loudly, they play 'who's the best?'
While otters just float, their naps are a jest.
A puffer fish yawned, quite the sleepy old fellow,
Dreaming of jelly with sprinkles, oh so yellow!

The tide brings new stories, each wave has a plot,
Like a fish who wore glasses — what a sight to spot!
With crabs who moonwalk on the wet sandy floor,
Dance parties erupt with a splash and a roar!

As shells share their secrets, beneath the sun's glow,
The laughter rolls high, just like the tide's flow.
Join in the fun, let the waves tickle your feet,
For the beach is a playground, where joy is complete.

Maritime Melodies

A sea bass composed on a floating old chair,
While seagulls perform with dramatic flair.
Crabs march in line, thinking they're the stars,
As waves tap their feet, like playful guitars.

The dolphin's aria, so bubbly and spry,
Turns shy little plankton all giggly and shy.
The mackerel swoons, in sparkly attire,
While sea urchins hum with a curious choir.

Squid inked a script, oh, the tales it can weave,
With tales of brave sailors who just wouldn't leave.
And starfish recite sonnets as night starts to fall,
Echoing giggles that bounce off the wall.

So come to the shore, let your troubles take flight,
In the sea's joyful chorus, everything's bright.
The maritime magic, a whimsical show,
With laughter and music, let the good vibes flow.

Whispers of the Tides

A crab in a tux, so suave and neat,
Dances on rocks, with two left feet.
The seagulls caw, they gossip and squawk,
As fish wear hats and pretend to walk.

Jellyfish jiggle with graceful glee,
Making fish laugh, like they're on TV.
A clam tells jokes, but they're rather shelly,
While turtles roll laughter, oh so silly.

A wave crashes in, with a splash and a grin,
Making seashells giggle, oh what a win!
Octopuses juggle with all of their arms,
While dolphins prank, with their slippery charms.

So join the fun, let's not turn blue,
When the tides are high, there's mischief to do.
Bring out your flippers, let's dance on the shore,
For laughter's the treasure we all should explore.

Songs Beneath the Waves

Bubbles floating up, like balloons in the air,
Fish sing in harmony, without a care.
The clams form a band, playing notes so bizarre,
While starfish groove, under the sea star.

A whale hums a tune, as it swims with style,
The shrimp add some beats, in their own funky file.
Sea cucumbers sway, in a slow-motion dance,
While rays fly around, in a gliding romance.

Splashing and swishing, they party all night,
A conch calls the crowd, "Let's dance in the light!"
With bubbles and laughter, they swirl around,
Creating a symphony from the oceanic sound.

So come and join in, don't be a wet blanket,
Grab your sea shoes, and let's go and prank it.
With rhythm and rhymes from the sea's gentle hymn,
We'll dance till the morning, our joy set to brim.

Melodies of Salt and Sea

Sardines in a choir, all singing off key,
While barnacles stomp, oh so joyfully.
The waves clap along, in a rhythmic embrace,
As gulls in their jackets, join the wild chase.

A lobster holds court, with a claw like a mic,
Telling tall tales, while shrimp ride a bike.
Starfish join in, making quite a fuss,
With their pointy arms, causing a fuss!

A sand crab tap dances, on the ocean floor,
Crabs counting the beats, while they all make the score.
With a wink and a nod, they dance all around,
Creating the melodies that vibrate the ground.

So if you're feeling blue, just jump in the brine,
Where the humor is fresh, and the laughter's divine.
From clam to the whale, it's a comedic sight,
In the throbbing salt sea, everything feels right.

Reflections on the Water's Surface

The sun shines down, on a skipping plankton,
Making them giggle, in their gelly hang-on.
A dolphin pops up, with an unexpected flair,
Waving at children, with joy in the air.

A fish with a grin, says, "I see you there!"
As seaweed shakes hands, with a comical stare.
The reflections of laughter ripple and wave,
A crustacean circus, it's mischief they crave.

With flip-flop fish, and octopus jokes,
The ocean seems full of hilarious folks.
Waves tickle toes, as you splash in surprise,
The water's a mirror, full of laughter and sighs.

So dip your toes in, and share a good chuckle,
For the sea holds secrets, like a playful puzzle.
With a wink and a splash, let your worries erase,
In the waters of fun, find your happy place.

Beneath a Blanket of Waves

A fish wore a hat, looked quite grand,
Said, "I'm the captain, don't you understand?"
He swam with a swagger, proud and bold,
While jellyfish giggled, their stories untold.

A crab in a coat was feeling quite fine,
He danced on the sand, sipping seaweed wine.
"Crustaceans unite! Let's throw a big bash!"
And the otters all laughed, diving in with a splash.

The Sea's Soliloquy

Seagulls debate on the best fish to eat,
While clams shout, "Hold on! We've got quite a beat!"
They tap on the shells, a dazzling show,
Puffing up bubbles with each rhythmic blow.

A starfish complained, feeling quite out of place,
"With five arms, I'm flashy, but can't win a race!"
The octopus laughed, revealing a grin,
"Just change your color; you always can win!"

Seabreeze Serenades

A dolphin sang songs with a voice so sweet,
While a clam threw a party to celebrate neat.
The sea turtles twirled, shells shining bright,
With crabs doing limbo, a hilarious sight.

But a whale belted out a horrible tune,
Prompting fish to hide; it was over too soon.
"Stop with your wailing! It's painful, dear mate!"
The octopus covered its ears, saying, "Too late!"

Lullabies from the Depths

An eel held a baby to rock in its arms,
Singing of coral and oceanic charms.
But the baby fish giggled, it just wouldn't sleep,
Said, "Send me to bed; the currents are deep!"

A crab read a story, his pinchers all tight,
While seaweed waved on, whispering "goodnight."
With tides rolling in, it was time for some rest,
And dreams filled with bubbles, oh, it was the best!

www.ingramcontent.com/pod-product-compliance
Lightning Source LLC
Chambersburg PA
CBHW060142230426
43661CB00003B/532